— BEGINNER'S —
BABY SIGN LANGUAGE

• SIGN & SING AT HOME •

SARA BINGHAM

Robert
ROSE

Library and Archives Canada Cataloguing in Publication

Title: Beginner's baby sign language : sign & sing at home / Sara Bingham.

Names: Bingham, Sara, author.

Description: Includes index.

Identifiers: Canadiana 2022027746X | ISBN 9780778807100 (softcover)

Subjects: LCSH: American Sign Language—Study and teaching (Early childhood) | LCSH: Nonverbal communication in infants. | LCSH: Interpersonal communication in infants.

Classification: LCC BF720.C65 B56 2023 | DDC 419/.700832—dc23

Disclaimer

This book is a general guide only and should never be a substitute for the skill, knowledge, and experience of a qualified professional dealing with the facts and circumstances of a particular case.

The information presented in this book is based on the research, training, and professional experience of the author, and is true and complete to the best of her knowledge. However, this book is intended only as an informative guide for those wishing to know more about baby signing; it is not intended to replace or countermand the advice given by the reader's personal physician or other health expert. Because each health situation is unique, the author and the publisher urge the reader to check with a qualified health-care professional before using any procedure where there is a question as to its appropriateness. The author and the publisher are not responsible for any adverse effects or consequences resulting from the use of the information in this book. It is the responsibility of the reader to consult a physician or other qualified health-care professional.

Design and production: PageWave Graphics Inc.

Illustrator: Jamie Villanueva

Cover and interior photographs: © Getty Images

Editor: Kathleen Fraser

Indexer: Gillian Watts

Published by Robert Rose Inc.

120 Eglinton Avenue East, Suite 800, Toronto, Ontario, Canada, M4P 1E2

Tel: (416) 322-6552 Fax: (416) 322-6936

www.robertrose.ca

Printed and bound in China

1 2 3 4 5 6 7 8 9 ESP 31 30 29 28 27 26 25 24 23

Dear Sara,

One month ago we were informed that our four-month-old grandchild needs hearing aids and that he will need to learn American Sign Language. I have been in search of children's books that include ASL. I was shocked to discover that few exist. I've also purchased a number of reference books. Two weeks ago I purchased your baby signing book. Of all the books that I have read, yours is by far the best. The drawings of each sign are simple, the faces of the man and woman signing are friendly, the description of the hand placement is easy to understand and your memory aids are definitely helpful. I want to thank you for making the world of ASL easier to navigate.

Sincerely, a grateful grandmother

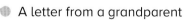 A letter from a grandparent

CONTENTS

CHAPTER 3

Family Signs 93

CHAPTER 4

Clothing and Routine Signs 121

CHAPTER 5

More Songs to Sign and Sing 153

Introduction

Welcome to the world of signing with your baby! This book will show you how, what and when to sign throughout your child's day. You can sign during mealtime, playtime, diaper-changing time and a host of other times in the day. In this introduction, we'll review what baby sign language is and the benefits of signing with your baby as well as why and how to sign the alphabet and beginning numbers in American Sign Language.

WHAT IS BABY SIGN LANGUAGE?

Baby sign language is the use of American Sign Language (ASL) signs with your baby or your beginning communicator. Another way to think of baby sign language is "keyword signing." Keyword signing uses signs to represent the main or key words in a sentence at the same time as the words are spoken.

I'm trained as a communicative disorders assistant. During my speech therapist days, I worked with adults and preschool children with developmental disabilities. It's with them that I learned about total communication and the concept of keyword signing. Using sign language with babies and toddlers lets them learn, play with and produce words using signs faster than they can produce spoken words alone.

When you speak as you typically would and add a visual representation of words, for example, by signing the key words in a sentence, your child has the opportunity to learn those words in a way they can easily produce at their stage of development. For example, if I say "Do you want some milk?" I show the sign for **MILK** because milk is the key word. Whatever number of signs you are comfortable signing with your baby works. Use the signs you know and are comfortable with.

THE BENEFITS OF SIGNING
with
YOUR BABY

- Signing allows your child to clearly communicate their thoughts.

- Signing allows your baby to direct the topic of conversation toward their interests.

- Signing reduces frustrations for your child, significantly lessening the terrible twos!

- Signing will not delay verbal language development; in fact, it will most likely increase it. Signing allows children to make mistakes, practice and learn more words earlier than their non-signing peers.

- Signing allows babies to make use of both their visual and kinesthetic skills. These are skills that develop earlier than auditory skills.

- Signing allows your baby to communicate with you about the books you share even when they don't have the ability to speak the words aloud. If you read a familiar book out loud to your baby and show the signs that you know while you are reading, your baby may actually take the book from you and sign the book back to you.

WHY AMERICAN SIGN LANGUAGE?

- American Sign Language (ASL) is the language of the Deaf in most of North America, except for Quebec, where they use LSQ (Quebec Sign Language, or Langue des Signes du Quèbec).

- ASL is the fourth most studied language at universities and colleges in the United States.

- ASL is a hand-based system. It doesn't interfere with the development of spoken words. For example, you can sign **FROG** and say "frog" at the same time. Some baby-gesturing programs teach babies to stick out their tongue to indicate the idea of frog. You can't do that and verbally say frog at the same time.

- ASL can be used beyond infancy. Your child is on a path to lifelong learning!

Using ASL can be beneficial for all young children, whether they are hearing, Deaf, hard of hearing or if they have a communicative disorder. I started signing with the young children I worked with because they had language delays. I signed with my hearing son because I wanted him to be able to communicate his wants and needs as soon as possible. In her kindergarten class, my hearing daughter signed with a little girl whose speech was delayed because she wanted to play with her.

WHY THE ASL ALPHABET?

Typically we are not going to be doing a lot of finger-spelling with your child. So why learn the alphabet? Learning to sign the alphabet (and some numbers) will help you learn a number of the handshapes that are needed to form ASL signs.

ASL signs are made up of five parts: handshape, body space, movement, palm orientation, and facial expression. For example, here are the parts that go into signing **APPLE.**

PARTS OF ASL SIGNS	FOR THE WORD APPLE
Handshape	Sign the letter **X** with your dominant hand, palm out
Body space	At the cheek
Movement	With a twist
Palm orientation	Starting with your palm facing out
Facial expression	With a neutral, happy or hungry facial expression

Knowing the components and characteristics of various signs will help you decipher your baby's possible sign approximations. I have found that babies and toddlers will generally get the body space and movement for a sign more or less correct, but may have difficulty with the handshape of a sign because of the finer motor skills needed for some hand shapes.

Having this knowledge will help you recognize your child's attempts at signing. For example, in the beginning, your child may sign **APPLE** using the correct body space and movement, but the handshape will be an approximation.

I've had many parents share that signing "The Alphabet Song" has helped them finish grocery shopping! As well, you can continue practicing the alphabet with your little ones well into the early years of school. It will help with their literacy skills.

We're almost ready to start. Here are a few things to keep in mind when you begin signing:

- Sign with your dominant hand. Your nondominant hand may be used as the base for some signs (see the sign for **BANANA**), or it may mimic your dominant hand (when signing **MORE**), or it may not be used at all (see the sign for **MILK**).

- Focus on signs for activities and items that are motivating for your baby.

- Don't be afraid to make mistakes, or to sign and sing!

- Have fun!

WHEN IS THE BEST TIME TO START TEACHING BABY SIGN LANGUAGE?

When the idea of signing with your baby was first introduced to the general public, around 1999, some resources recommended that parents wait until their babies were six months of age before starting. My son was born in 2000, and that's what I did. Now, knowing what I know about using sign language to encourage language development, I would have started signing with my son earlier.

I posed this question on one of my social media channels, and parents from across North America shared a range of starting ages, from birth to 11 months. Claire-Lise, in Toronto, started signing with her son when he was a few weeks old and she reported that by 16 months he had more than 50 signs! Another signing mom, Christi from St. Louis, started signing with her little one when he was 11 months old, and at 18 months, he had 130 words!

Most babies will start signing back to you between 9 and 11 months, but they may understand what you sign to them even before that. You may sign **MILK** when your baby is hungry and he'll calm down. You might sign **BATH** to your little one who loves bath time and she'll get excited. Sign language will help you understand your baby before they can speak and it can also help your baby understand you. The best day to start signing with your little one is today!

HOW TO START SIGNING
with
YOUR BABY

You'll want to start with ASL signs for words that are really motivating for your little one. A great first sign to start with for any baby is the sign for **MILK.**

→ **SIGN IT BEFORE**

Every time you say the word "milk," show your baby the sign for **MILK** as well. This will help your baby associate the gesture or sign with the word "milk."

→ **SIGN IT DURING**

While your baby is nursing or drinking from a bottle in your arms, you can show the sign again while you talk about it. For example, say, "Yes, you're having your milk," and sign **MILK** when you say "milk."

→ **SIGN IT AFTER**

When your baby is finished nursing or drinking from a bottle (and if they are still awake!), show the sign again and say the words, "Your **MILK** is all done. You're done with your **MILK**."

What else is motivating for your baby? Choose other signs for things your baby is most motivated by and interested in. For my son that was words from songs and books, like **STAR** and **FISH**; for my daughter, that was food signs, like **EAT** and **MORE**.

→ **START WITH 10 TO 12 SIGNS**

Choose about five or six signs for things your baby really likes, for example, **MILK**. Add five or six signs for things that happen a number of times in your baby's day, for example, **CHANGE**.

Your baby won't be confused if you show them more than 10 signs at a time. If you like, you can sign every word you say. But if you are just beginning signing yourself, add more when you are comfortable using them regularly, and then add more!

HOW TO USE
this
BOOK

With this book, you'll be able to learn 112 ASL signs. The vocabulary and signs have been chosen especially for new parents, expecting parents, grandparents, caregivers, educators, therapists and child-care workers to use. The book is for anyone who wants to connect with the children in their lives and who is interested in early language development.

The signs, vocabulary, songs and language development strategies that I've included are all ones that have been taught in a WeeHands Sign and Sing at Home class for the past 20 years.

Especially if you are a new parent, focus on showing your child signs for things that are of high interest to your baby, such as milk, water or fish, as well as signs for activities that happen frequently throughout the day, including bath, change and eat.

Don't be overwhelmed by the number of signs included in this book. You can sign at home with your baby using whatever number of signs you are comfortable with and will use regularly. Once you are consistently using those signs, and as your baby's interests and routines expand, add more signs.

What if I learned that sign differently?

Just as words in spoken languages vary from region to region (such as "soda" and "pop"), words in sign languages can vary as well. If you've learned a sign from the Deaf community in your area that is different from what's shown here, use the version that your Deaf community uses. Neither version is wrong; they are just different.

Take note, however, that if you've learned a version of a sign that solely relies on the mouth (like making a puckering motion for your lips to represent "fish"), this is likely not from ASL. I encourage you to use ASL signs with your child because they allow you to also say the word at the same time!

Why not sign the entire sentence?

If you know signs for a whole sentence that you want to use, use them. Keep in mind that ASL word order and grammar is different from English word order.

However, if you are just starting out with sign language, I encourage you to use keyword signing with your baby. For example, you may verbally say, "Do you want milk?" paired with the single sign for **MILK**. This puts the emphasis on the most important concept in the sentence and gives your baby the idea of that concept in a way they can both hear and see.

Let's start signing!

THE ALPHABET IN ASL

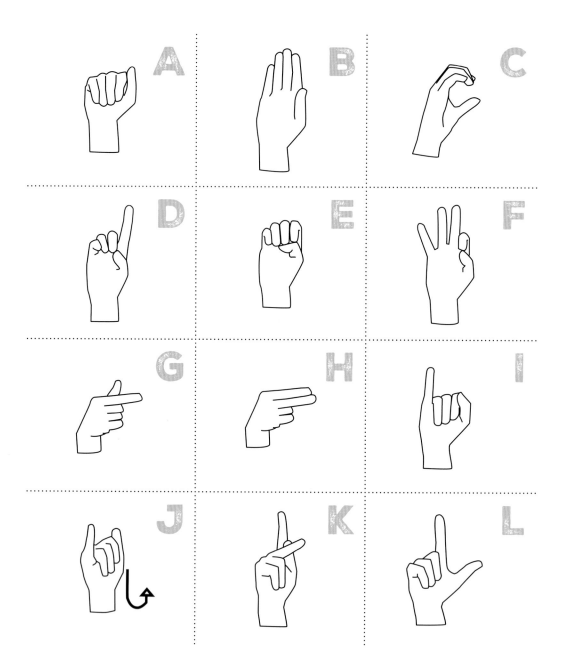

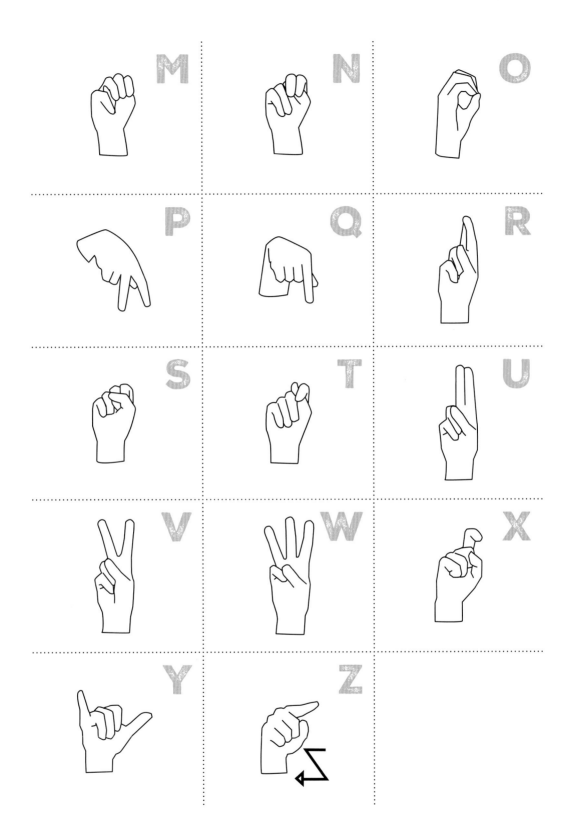

NUMBERS 1 TO 10 IN ASL

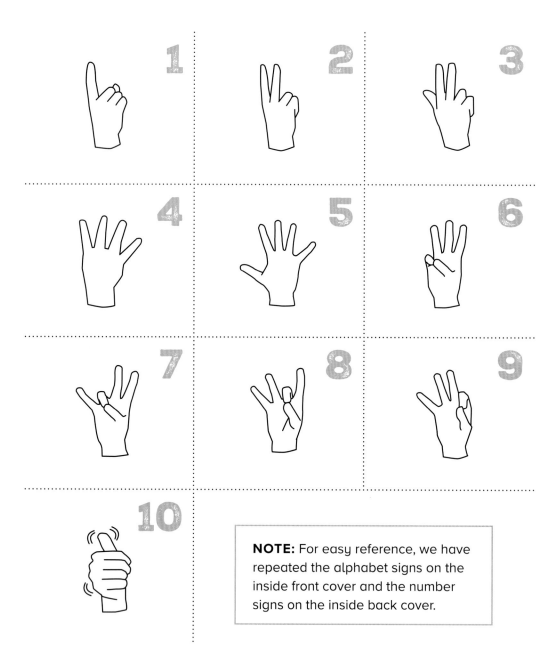

NOTE: For easy reference, we have repeated the alphabet signs on the inside front cover and the number signs on the inside back cover.

HANDSHAPES BEGIN
with
ALPHABET AND NUMBER SIGNS

Keep in mind that the handshape for a sign for a word often begins with a sign for a letter of the alphabet. For example, when you sign **MILK**, you begin with an **S** handshape.

Some begin with number signs; for example, the **5** shape is used to sign **MOTHER** and **FATHER**.

Also, some handshapes can be slightly modified. For example, the **O** handshape can be flat, open or closed. **MORE** begin with what is called a flat **O** shape, where you flatten the top fingers of an **O** shape. Similarly, you can sign a relaxed **5** shape, which is a little looser than the usual **5** handshape.

For some words, like **JUICE**, the handshape is the letter the word starts with — in this case, the **J** shape. Once you learn the alphabet and number signs, you will have a head start on these other signs.

Tips for signing at home

Practice singing and signing "The Alphabet Song" (see page 169) with your child. You can start by signing only the letters and then add the other words as you learn them. Share signing the song with other caregivers too. Your baby will enjoy the attention and may be fascinated with what you're doing with your hands!

CHAPTER 1

Signs to Start With

LET'S START SIGNING! Throughout this book, you'll be shown signs for words that are typically the first words for any baby, whether signed or spoken. In this chapter, you'll learn eight core signs to use with your baby along with a fun song, plus more signs to use during one of the activities that you'll probably be doing most with your baby — diaper changing. Think of the words in this first chapter as your foundation.

For each sign, I'll explain how the sign is made describing the hand shape, body space and movement you'll use. For most signs, I'll also share memory aids to help you understand the way the sign is made. I'll also share when to use the sign and, for most signs, what to look for when your baby is first starting to use the sign.

Most babies, when they first start signing, use the correct body space and the correct movement for the sign, but the handshape will be off. Your baby may not yet have the fine motor skills to make the sign just as an adult would. When you know this, you can look for their approximate version of the sign and then respond to the attempt made. For example, you may give them what they asked for and then model the sign again for your baby. (Some of the signs in this book don't note "what to look for." That information is included only when a baby might typically make an approximation of a sign and not when they typically make a sign the same way an adult would.)

Use your dominant hand to do most of the movement when you are making the signs shown. For example, when you sign **MILK**, if you are right-handed, make the sign with your right hand. If you are left-handed, make the sign with your left hand. Some signs, such as the sign for **MORE**, are made with both hands doing the exact same thing. Other signs, such as **CLEAN**, use your nondominant hand as the base, while your dominant hand still does the movement.

Don't worry if you don't produce the signs perfectly yet. Your baby won't mind. What's most important to them is that they get to spend time with you. Also, don't worry if you can't sign as quickly as you speak. That's to be expected. As a beginning signer, when you sign and speak, your speech will slow down. Slowing down your speech and showing your baby a visual representation of the key words in your sentences will help your child learn language.

You can start showing your baby these signs to start with as soon as you are comfortable, no matter what your baby's age. I've seen some parents start to sign with their babies as soon as they were born. Other parents begin signing with their babies when they are 10 months old. Most babies will sign their first sign back to you between the 9 and 11 months of age.

Remember that every baby is different. Well before your baby signs back to you, she will most definitely show you that she understands what you're signing to her. She'll get excited when you sign **MILK** or she'll try to roll away when you sign **DIAPER**. Whatever your child's age, the best time to start signing with your baby is today!

With most babies, the order of development usually follows the same pattern. I found that as my own children learned to sign, first they watched my hands, then they laughed or smiled at my movements. This they followed by imitating my hands, which sometimes looked like them just waving their hands around.

My son signed back to me when he was 9 months of age. I was reading and signing an animal board book to him to keep him amused during his lunch. When we got to a page that had a photo of a goldfish on it, I said and signed **FISH**, then paused. He smiled and signed **FISH** back to me!

My daughter, my second born, signed back to me when she was 11 months old. She was a little one who got into cupboards, banged on the television screen and in general wanted to play with things that she shouldn't. I'm not proud of it but I said and signed **NO** to her a lot her first year. One sunny afternoon she was crawling over to a large plant that I had in the kitchen, when she stopped, smiled at me, signed **NO** and immediately started digging in that plant.

What I love about both these stories is that Joshua's first sign was to comment about something in a book that we were reading together and Sabrina's first sign was to clearly joke with and tease me. Often we think a first sign should be something that a baby wants, like **MILK**, and that may be the case. Your baby also wants to share experiences and attention with you. Keep that in mind when you are choosing signs to show them throughout your day together.

Use these first signs shown in this chapter throughout the day with your baby as often as you can. Sign and sing "The Alphabet Song" and the "Change Your Diaper" song as often as you remember throughout the day.

We've included space for you to record the date that you start showing your baby each sign and the date that your baby started making the sign. If you have any questions about signing with your baby, toddler or preschool child, join our free community online here: https://weehands.community.

more

HANDSHAPE
Flat **O** shape with both hands, fingertips and thumb touching

BODY SPACE
At chest level

MOVEMENT
Tap your fingertips together.

MEMORY AID
It looks as if you are adding two things together to make more.

WHEN TO USE THE SIGN
MORE is usually used as a question, as in "Do you want more?" Say the word and show the sign for **MORE** when your baby has finished eating something but you know they'll still be hungry. You might also gently take something away from your baby and, if your baby reaches for the item, pause and show the sign for **MORE**. Don't do this if it frustrates your baby.

WHAT TO LOOK FOR
When your baby first attempts to sign **MORE**, it might look like they're clapping.

Date introduced:

Date produced:

....

....

eat (food)

HANDSHAPE
O shape with dominant hand, palm facing you

BODY SPACE
At your mouth

MOVEMENT
Tap your mouth once with your fingertips; tap twice for the noun **FOOD**.

MEMORY AID
It looks as if you are bringing food to your mouth.

WHEN TO USE THE SIGN
Say the word and show this sign before and while your baby is eating. Use the sign **EAT** when you're eating, any pets are eating and even when pretending to feed a doll.

WHAT TO LOOK FOR
Your baby may tap his open hand against his mouth.

Date introduced:

Date produced:

....

....

finish

HANDSHAPE
5 shape with both hands, palms facing you

BODY SPACE
At chest level

MOVEMENT
Turn hands at wrists away from the body, ending with palms facing out.

MEMORY AID
It looks as if you are brushing something away from you.

WHEN TO USE THE SIGN
Say the word "finished" or "all done," and show the **FINISH** sign when a food item or an activity is finished.

WHAT TO LOOK FOR
Your baby may be flapping or waving one or both of her hands when she tries to make this sign at first.

Date introduced:

Date produced:

....

....

milk

HANDSHAPE
S shape with dominant hand, palm facing you

BODY SPACE
At chest level

MOVEMENT
Open and close your hand several times. (This can also be signed with two hands.)

MEMORY AID
This sign looks a little like you are milking a cow with one hand.

WHEN TO USE THE SIGN
Show this sign to your baby whenever you say the word "milk" as well as before, during and after they drink milk.

WHAT TO LOOK FOR
It might look like your baby is waving or flicking their hand back and forth when they first attempt to make this sign.

Date introduced:

Date produced:

....

....

cookie

HANDSHAPE
A **5** shape bent as if a claw, with dominant hand; **B** shape with other hand, palm up

BODY SPACE
At chest level

MOVEMENT
Touch the fingertips of your dominant hand to the palm of your other hand and twist.

MEMORY AID
Twist as if using a cookie-cutter.

WHEN TO USE THE SIGN
Say the word and show this sign to your baby just before and while she's eating a cookie.

WHAT TO LOOK FOR
When your baby attempts to sign this word, it might look as if she is squishing her hands together.

Date introduced:

Date produced:

....

please

HANDSHAPE
Open **B** shape, thumb is extended, with dominant hand, palm facing body

BODY SPACE
At chest level

MOVEMENT
Move your hand in a circle over your chest.

MEMORY AID
You are rubbing a circle over your heart because you really want something. Do this with an appropriate facial expression.

WHEN TO USE THE SIGN
Use this sign with your baby when they are using one-word signs to tell you what they want. For example, when your baby signs **MILK**, you can model the phrase **MILK PLEASE** to them. Don't force your child to sign **PLEASE** before they get something.

WHAT TO LOOK FOR
It may look like your baby is rubbing or patting his chest when he signs **PLEASE**.

Date introduced:

Date produced:

....

....

no

HANDSHAPE
3 shape with dominant hand, palm out

BODY SPACE
At shoulder level

MOVEMENT
Open and close the fingers of your dominant hand, repeating the action, and shaking your head "no" (from side to side) at the same time.

MEMORY AID
When you repeat the gestures, you are quickly finger-spelling **N** and **O**.

WHEN TO USE THE SIGN
Use the sign anytime you say the word "no." Do this with an appropriate facial expression.

Date introduced:

Date produced:

....

....

time

HANDSHAPE
Bent **1** shape, dominant hand

BODY SPACE
Just below chest level

MOVEMENT
Use the pointer finger of your dominant hand to tap your other wrist twice.

MEMORY AID
It looks as if you are tapping your watch.

WHEN TO USE THE SIGN
Show this sign to your baby when you are signing and singing the "Change Your Diaper" song.

WHAT TO LOOK FOR
It may look like your baby is knocking his fist on his wrist.

Date introduced:

Date produced:

....

now

HANDSHAPE
Bent **B** shape with both hands apart and palms up. This sign can also be made with **Y** shapes.

BODY SPACE
At chest level

MOVEMENT
Bending your **B** shape at your fingers, lower both hands at the same time.

MEMORY AID
There isn't really a memory aid for this abstract concept. Depending on the context, your movement may be sharper.

WHEN TO USE THE SIGN
Use this sign when singing the "Change Your Diaper" song and whenever you say the word "now" in everyday speech.

Date introduced:

Date produced:

....

....

diaper

HANDSHAPE
H shape with both hands, palms facing body

BODY SPACE
At waist

MOVEMENT
Open and close your pointer (index) finger and thumb together twice.

MEMORY AID
It looks as if you are showing or snapping the diaper pins or snaps on a cloth diaper.

WHEN TO USE THE SIGN
Say the word and show this sign to your baby when bringing a diaper to them and while changing their diaper.

WHAT TO LOOK FOR
It may look like your baby is patting herself on the belly or hips.

Date introduced:

....

Date produced:

....

change

HANDSHAPE
A shape with both hands, palms facing each other

BODY SPACE
At chest level

MOVEMENT
Starting with your closed hands one over the other, twist your hands so they change position; the one on top moves to the bottom.

MEMORY AID
It looks like your hands are changing position.

WHEN TO USE THE SIGN
Say the word and show your baby this sign before a diaper change and while you're singing the song "Change Your Diaper."

WHAT TO LOOK FOR
It may look like your baby is rolling her hands together when she first attempts this sign.

Date introduced:

Date produced:

....

....

wet (soft)

HANDSHAPE
Relaxed **5** shape with both hands apart and palms up

BODY SPACE
At chest level

MOVEMENT
Move both hands gently down and into flat **O** shapes, closing your fingers to your thumbs.

MEMORY AID
It looks as if you are holding something that is dripping wet.

WHEN TO USE THE SIGN
Show your baby this sign and say the word when touching anything wet. This is also the sign for **SOFT**. Use it for "mush" in the song "On Top of Spaghetti."

WHAT TO LOOK FOR
It might look as if your baby is waving both her hands.

Date introduced:

Date produced:

....

....

dry

HANDSHAPE
X shape with dominant hand, palm down

BODY SPACE
At your chin

MOVEMENT
Move your hand across your chin from left to right, or right to left, depending on which hand is your dominant hand.

MEMORY AID
Do this as if wiping something wet off your chin.

WHEN TO USE THE SIGN
Use this sign and say the word when drying off something that's wet as well as when singing the "Change Your Diaper" song.

WHAT TO LOOK FOR
It may look like your baby or toddler is wiping her chin.

Date introduced:

Date produced:

....

....

dirty

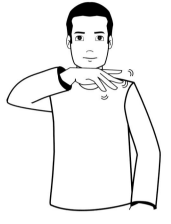

HANDSHAPE
5 shape with dominant hand, palm down

BODY SPACE
Under your chin

MOVEMENT
With your hand under your chin, wiggle your fingers.

MEMORY AID
It looks as if you know your chin is dirty.

WHEN TO USE THE SIGN
Show your baby this sign and say the word when touching or looking at anything dirty. When signing and singing the "Change Your Diaper" song, you can also mime a "smelly" gesture for the word dirty.

WHAT TO LOOK FOR
Your baby might make this sign just by placing his hand under his chin.

Date introduced:

....

Date produced:

....

clean (nice)

HANDSHAPE
B shape with both hands, palms facing each other

BODY SPACE
At chest level

MOVEMENT
Wipe your dominant hand across your other hand from your wrist to the tips of your fingers.

MEMORY AID
It looks as if you are wiping a table clean.

WHEN TO USE THE SIGN
Say the word and show this sign when it's time to clean up or when you want to say that something is clean. It also used as the sign for **NICE**. (In some daycare settings, this sign is sometimes mistakenly used for the word "finished.")

Date introduced:

....

Date produced:

....

fish

HANDSHAPE
B shape with dominant hand, palm facing you

BODY SPACE
At chest level

MOVEMENT
Move your dominant hand across your body while bending your wrist left and right.

MEMORY AID
Your hand imitates the movement of a swimming fish.

WHEN TO USE THE SIGN
Say the word and show this sign when looking at pictures of fish, having fish for dinner or talking about the family pet goldfish.

Date introduced:

....

Date produced:

....

goodbye

HANDSHAPE
B shape with dominant hand, palm facing out

BODY SPACE
At head or shoulder level

MOVEMENT
Bend your fingers up and down.

MEMORY AID
It looks as if you are waving goodbye.

WHEN TO USE THE SIGN
Use this sign when saying goodbye to your baby or anyone else. When you say it, sign it.

Date introduced:

Date produced:

....

....

Tips for signing at home

Practice signing **MORE**, **EAT**, **COOKIE**, **MILK**, **FINISHED**, **CHANGE** and **PLEASE** with your child. Share these words with other caregivers too. Whenever you say any of these words, remember to sign them!

Start thinking about a list of words for your child that includes words for things and actions that they will see a lot and do a lot, like eat. All babies are different, and have different items they like to play with or eat. Many of the signs for these words will appear throughout this book. We want to make sure that you have a list of at least 10 to 15 words that are important to your baby that you can sign throughout the day.

SIGN AND SING AT HOME

Sign and sing the "Change Your Diaper" song to your baby before and during (if you can) diaper change time. Sign and sing this song to your baby before and during (if you can) diaper change time. You can also sign and sing this song with your older baby or toddler while pretending to change the diaper of a doll or stuffed bear. Visit our online community, https://weehands.community, to see a cute video of this song to share with your baby.

Sign the number of words in the song that you are comfortable with. To start you may only sign the word **DIAPER**, and then **DIAPER** and **CHANGE**. Add more signs as you get comfortable. You'll also see in the lyrics that we've interpreted the concept of a "full" diaper using the sign for **DIRTY**. Or you could also use a gesture that indicates "smelly"! You will have lots of opportunities to practice!

Change Your Diaper

It's **TIME** to **CHANGE** your **DIAPER** 'cause it's **WET**,

Oh, it's **TIME** to **CHANGE** your **DIAPER** 'cause it's **WET**.

It's **TIME** to **CHANGE** your **DIAPER**,

It's **TIME** to **CHANGE** your **DIAPER**

Oh, it's **TIME** to **CHANGE** your **DIAPER** 'cause it's **WET**.

It's **TIME** to **CHANGE** your **DIAPER** 'cause it's full (**DIRTY**),

Oh, it's **TIME** to **CHANGE** your **DIAPER** 'cause it's full.

It's **TIME** to **CHANGE** your **DIAPER**,

It's **TIME** to **CHANGE** your **DIAPER**

Oh, it's **TIME** to **CHANGE** your **DIAPER** 'cause it's full.

Oh, we just **CHANGE**d your **DIAPER**, **NOW** it's **DRY**,

Oh, we just **CHANGE**d your **DIAPER**, **NOW** it's **DRY**.

Oh, we just **CHANGE**d your **DIAPER**,

Now you're **CLEAN** and **DRY**.

Oh, we just **CHANGE**d your **DIAPER**, **NOW** it's **DRY**.

TIME

CHANGE

DIAPER

WET

DIRTY

NOW

CLEAN

DRY

CHAPTER 2

Food Signs

I ENCOURAGE YOU to sign at least 20 to 30 times a day with your baby, using a variety of signs for activities and items that are of interest to your little one. Babies learn words more readily when parents look at and name objects that their child already finds motivating. With that in mind, I encourage you to generate a list of at least 10 to 12 signs that you can use throughout the day with your child. Break this list down as follows:

- Half of these signs are about something that is highly motivating to your child.

- Half of these signs represent frequently occurring activities.

Mealtime is a wonderful time to introduce signs and food vocabulary to your child. That's because the words are typically very motivating and the activity happens consistently and frequently throughout the day. Mealtime can be an activity for great learning and bonding!

As you get more comfortable, you can add more and more signs to the list you use. We don't limit our speech when we communicate with babies, so you don't have to limit the number of signs you use.

Always verbally say the word while you are signing it. This gives your little learner both auditory and visual input about the concepts they are learning.

Food is often a motivator for little ones, so starting off with signs for **MILK, MORE** and **EAT** is a good idea! To these, add a number of signs for other items that are highly motivating to your little one, including food signs.

During mealtime with your little one, offer small portions. Between bites, pause and wait to see what he does to indicate that he wants more. Does he look toward you expectantly and open his mouth? Does he lean toward you and hold out his hand? Does he reach for the food item, look at it and look at you? These are all ways that early communicators may try to get across their message. In this case, the message is "Feed me!"

Recognize and respond to how your little one is communicating now and model the correct sign for the food item. Pausing between bites creates opportunities for your little one to sign back. If your baby doesn't sign back yet, keep modeling the signs and creating opportunities for them to sign back to you.

BEFORE, DURING AND AFTER

Model food signs before you give a food item to your little one, for example, "Here comes the **BANANA**."

Model food signs during mealtime for your little one, for example, "You're eating the **BANANA**. It's **GOOD**!"

Model the food item after it's gone, for example, "The **BANANA**'s **FINISH**ed!"

"Signing was an extremely helpful tool with my daughter particularly when she could sign what she wanted without having to cry."

—JULIA LAGMAN

Signing while reading

When you are sharing a book with your little one, you will want to keep the book and your signs visible. You've only got two hands, though, so how can you do that?

Some parents use a cookbook stand to hold a book up and open so that they can sign what's on each page. You can also sit side by side on the couch or on the floor and make many of your signs right on the book itself.

Most board books for small children will stay open. Put the book on a pillow or propped up on a table so that your baby can see the book and your signs.

When your baby is in her high chair, you can put the book propped on the edge of her tray or flat on the tray if you don't mind reading upside-down!

You don't have to sign every word. Start with key words, nouns and verbs. Do what you are comfortable with and have fun!

Choose books with repetitive language and familiar vocabulary. You'll soon not even have to look at the words, because you've read your baby's favorite books so often you have the words memorized!

Keep in mind where you and your baby like to sit and have conversations. Take your books there. Just be sure she can see your face, your signs and the book.

When my son was a baby he was rarely motivated by mealtime. I had to read to him to keep him interested in any mealtime activity. I had to learn how to keep the books from getting covered in food too!

Use the food signs shown in this chapter during mealtime for you and your baby and when you come across the words in any books you read together. Sign and sing the "Baby's Eating" song as well as "On Top of Spaghetti" at mealtime and whenever you want throughout the day.

juice

HANDSHAPE
J shape with dominant hand

BODY SPACE
At your cheek

MOVEMENT
With your pinky (little) finger extended, draw a **J** shape.

MEMORY AID
It looks as if you are drawing a **J** at your cheek.

WHEN TO USE THE SIGN
Say the word and show this sign to your baby whenever he is drinking juice.

WHAT TO LOOK FOR
When your baby first makes this sign, it may look like he is tapping his mouth. Whenever your baby makes an approximation like this, say the word, model the way you would sign it and respond to him as soon as you can.

Date introduced:

Date produced:

....

....

banana

HANDSHAPE

O shape with dominant hand; **1** shape with other hand

BODY SPACE

At chest level

MOVEMENT

Move the fingertips of your dominant hand up and down the pointer finger of your other hand.

MEMORY AID

It looks a little like you are peeling a banana.

WHEN TO USE THE SIGN

Say the word and show your baby the sign for **BANANA** before and after you peel, cut up or mash banana. Show as well when you or baby is eating a banana.

WHAT TO LOOK FOR

Your baby may use a similar body space and movement when attempting this sign but their handshape may be different; for example, they may use their whole hands for both movements.

Date introduced:

Date produced:

....

....

cheese

HANDSHAPE
With the heel of dominant hand in a **C** shape on heel of other hand

BODY SPACE
Just below chest level

MOVEMENT
Twist your dominant hand on your other hand several times.

MEMORY AID
It looks as if you are squeezing the whey from curds to make cheese.

WHEN TO USE THE SIGN
Say the word and show your child this sign whenever he or you are eating cheese.

WHAT TO LOOK FOR
When your baby first makes this sign, it may look as if he is mashing his hands together or clapping.

Date introduced: Date produced:

....

water

HANDSHAPE

W shape with dominant hand, palm facing out

BODY SPACE

At your mouth

MOVEMENT

Tap your hand in a **W** shape twice at your chin

MEMORY AID

W is for water, something you can drink.

WHEN TO USE THE SIGN

Say the word and show your baby this sign whenever she or you are drinking or playing with water.

WHAT TO LOOK FOR

Your baby may first make this sign the way you would, but without a **W** handshape. It may look like she is patting her mouth with her full hand or tapping it with one finger.

Date introduced:

Date produced:

....

....

apple

HANDSHAPE
X shape with dominant hand

BODY SPACE
At your cheek

MOVEMENT
Twist the knuckle of your pointer finger back and forth at your cheek twice.

MEMORY AID
It looks as if you are twisting an apple stem at the "apple" of your cheek.

WHEN TO USE THE SIGN
Sign and say **APPLE** to your baby when he is eating applesauce or an apple and when you see an apple at the store, on a tree, at home or in a book.

WHAT TO LOOK FOR
When first making this sign, your baby may tap his cheek with his full hand or twist his pointer finger near his cheek.

Date introduced:

Date produced:

....

cereal

HANDSHAPE
X shape with dominant hand; **B** shape with the other hand, palm up

BODY SPACE
At chest level

MOVEMENT
Brush your finger making an **X** shape toward the inside of the elbow of your other arm twice.

MEMORY AID
It looks as if you are cutting down grain with a scythe to make cereal.

WHEN TO USE THE SIGN
Say the word and show your baby this sign when eating cereal of any kind. Note: You'll often see variations of this sign in different geographical regions.

WHAT TO LOOK FOR
You may see your child moving their hand on their forearm or near their elbow, especially around or just before mealtime.

Date introduced:

Date produced

....

peas

HANDSHAPE
1 shape with both hands, palms facing the body

BODY SPACE
At chest level

MOVEMENT
If your right hand is your dominant hand, keep your left hand pointing to the right and bounce the tip of your right pointer finger across your left pointer finger. (Do in reverse if you are left-handed.)

MEMORY AID
It looks as if you are pointing to little peas in a pea pod.

WHEN TO USE THE SIGN
Say the word and show this sign to your baby before, while and after she is eating peas.

WHAT TO LOOK FOR
It is very cute when your child starts to use this sign. If they really like peas, they may point to their hand very seriously!

Date introduced:

Date produced:

....

....

cracker

HANDSHAPE
A shape with dominant hand

BODY SPACE
At the opposite elbow

MOVEMENT
With fists closed, tap the outside of your opposite elbow twice.

MEMORY AID
Imagine you are cracking a large sheet of crackers on your elbow to break them up (or crushing a small package of crackers to put in your soup).

WHEN TO USE THE SIGN
Say the word and show this sign to your baby whenever he (or anyone) is about to eat or is eating crackers.

WHAT TO LOOK FOR
Your baby may try to make this sign by hitting his fist on his other hand or his wrist. Whenever your baby makes an approximation like this, say the word, model the sign the way you would sign it and respond to him as soon as you can.

Date introduced:

Date produced:

....

....

spaghetti

HANDSHAPE
I shape with both hands, fingertips touching, palms facing the body

BODY SPACE
At chest level

MOVEMENT
Begin with pinky fingers touching and move your hands apart while rotating them up and down.

MEMORY AID
Think of twirling or curvy pasta.

WHEN TO USE THE SIGN
Use this sign whenever you say "spaghetti," "pasta" or "noodles."

WHAT TO LOOK FOR
Your baby may first make this sign using her pointer fingers and not her pinky fingers.

Date introduced:

Date produced:

....

....

meat

HANDSHAPE

F shape with dominant hand; open **B** shape with other hand, palm facing you

BODY SPACE

At chest level

MOVEMENT

Use your dominant hand to grasp the skin between the thumb and pointer finger on your other hand, shaking hands slightly.

MEMORY AID

Think of meat hanging on a hook in a butcher shop.

WHEN TO USE THE SIGN

Say the word and show this sign to your baby whenever he is eating or about to eat chicken, beef, pork or any type of meat.

WHAT TO LOOK FOR

When your baby tries to make this sign, it may look like she is grabbing her hand or her arm. Whenever your baby makes an approximation like this, say the word, model the sign the way you'd sign it and respond to her as soon as you can.

Date introduced: Date produced:

....

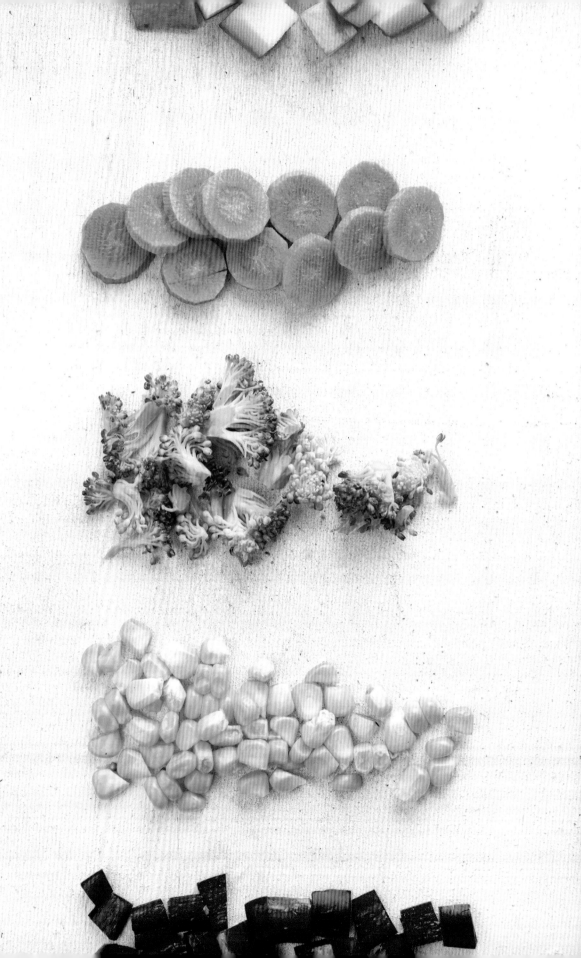

vegetable

HANDSHAPE
V shape with dominant hand, palm facing out

BODY SPACE
At your cheek

MOVEMENT
Twist your dominant hand forward from the wrist, keeping your pointer finger in contact with your cheek.

MEMORY AID
It looks like a V for vegetable at the side of your mouth.

WHEN TO USE THE SIGN
Use the sign when eating vegetables and when singing the "Five Laughing Babies" song.

WHAT TO LOOK FOR
Your baby might make an approximation of this sign by making some sort of movement at their cheek, patting or pointing to their cheek.

Date introduced:

Date produced:

....

....

baby

HANDSHAPE
B shape with both hands

BODY SPACE
Between chest and stomach level

MOVEMENT
With palms facing up and arms overlapping, rock your arms back and forth.

MEMORY AID
It looks like you are rocking a baby in your arms.

WHEN TO USE THE SIGN
Say and sign **BABY** whenever you see another baby as well as when you see a toy baby or a doll.

WHAT TO LOOK FOR
When your baby first makes this sign, it may look like she is hugging herself and rocking.

Date introduced:

Date produced:

....

....

drink

HANDSHAPE
C shape with dominant hand, palm
facing you

BODY SPACE
At the mouth

MOVEMENT
Tilt your hand up.

MEMORY AID
It looks as if you are tipping a cup to
take a drink.

WHEN TO USE THE SIGN
Say the word and show this sign to your baby
whenever you, your baby or your pet is drinking something.

WHAT TO LOOK FOR
It may look like your baby is tapping her mouth when she first
makes this sign.

Date introduced:

Date produced:

....

....

hungry

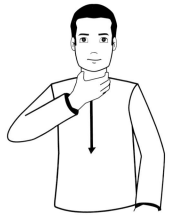

HANDSHAPE
C shape with dominant hand, palm facing you

BODY SPACE
Just below your neck

MOVEMENT
Move your hand downward firmly one time.

MEMORY AID
You are indicating your throat, where you would like food to go.

WHEN TO USE THE SIGN
Use this sign whenever you say the word "hungry," especially when you notice your baby might be hungry.

WHAT TO LOOK FOR
Your baby might approximate this sign by using a different handshape, for example, a **1** shape (which is the sign for **THIRSTY**). If you see this, offer them a choice between a food item and a drink. If your baby points to the food item, model signing and saying "You're **HUNGRY**. You want a **COOKIE** because you are **HUNGRY**."

Date introduced:

Date produced:

....

....

table

HANDSHAPE

Open **B** shape with the thumb extended, with both hands, palms facing down; dominant forearm on top of other forearm

BODY SPACE

At chest level

MOVEMENT

Stack your forearms, tapping the top of your bottom forearm a few times.

MEMORY AID

It looks as if you are resting both arms on a table.

WHEN TO USE THE SIGN

Use this sign when saying the word "table" during mealtime or playtime as well as when you are singing "On Top of Spaghetti."

WHAT TO LOOK FOR

It may look like your baby is making a clapping motion when she first tries to use this sign.

Date introduced:

....

Date produced:

....

floor

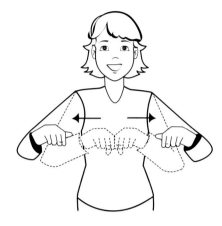

HANDSHAPE
B shape with both hands, palms down and pointer fingers touching

BODY SPACE
At chest level

MOVEMENT
Move your hands apart at the same time.

MEMORY AID
It looks as if your hands are moving across a flat floor.

WHEN TO USE THE SIGN
Use this sign when saying the word "floor" during playtime as well as when you are singing "On Top of Spaghetti."

WHAT TO LOOK FOR
It may look like your baby or toddler is swinging their arms out wide when they first use this sign.

Date introduced:

Date produced:

....

door

HANDSHAPE

B shape with both hands, palms facing out

BODY SPACE

At chest level, with the thumbs of both hands touching

MOVEMENT

Twist your dominant hand backward so that the palm of your hand is facing you.

MEMORY AID

It is as if one side of a set of French doors is opening inward towards you.

WHEN TO USE THE SIGN

Use this sign when you open or close a door to a room, a cabinet or a vehicle.

WHAT TO LOOK FOR

Your child may use a much larger motion than you do when she first uses this sign.

Date introduced: *Date produced:*

....

my (mine)

HANDSHAPE
Open **B** shape, thumb is extended, with dominant hand, palm facing you

BODY SPACE
At chest level

MOVEMENT
Tap your chest firmly once.

MEMORY AID
It looks as if you are claiming possession.

WHEN TO USE THE SIGN
Use this sign whenever you say the words "my" or "mine."

Date introduced:

....

Date produced:

....

good

HANDSHAPE

B shape with dominant hand, fingertips at the mouth; **B** shape with other hand, palm up

BODY SPACE

Dominant hand at mouth, other hand at chest level

MOVEMENT

Touch your chin with your dominant hand, then move it down onto your other hand.

MEMORY AID

It looks as if you have something that tastes good and you want to keep it or share it with others.

WHEN TO USE THE SIGN

Say and sign **GOOD** during mealtime when you are tasting or serving something delicious. Also use this sign when saying good morning or good night. Try to stay away from labeling behavior as good — or bad.

WHAT TO LOOK FOR

When your child first uses this sign, it may look like she is blowing kisses!

Date introduced:

Date produced:

....

garden (version 1)

HANDSHAPE

Flat **O** shape with dominant hand;
C shape with other hand

BODY SPACE

Just below chest level

MOVEMENT

Move your dominant hand up
through your other hand and open it
into a **5** shape. Shift your arms slightly
to the other side and repeat.

MEMORY AID

This shows more than one plant growing beside another. With just
one movement, this is the sign for **PLANT**.

WHEN TO USE THE SIGN

Use this sign when going to or playing in the garden.

WHAT TO LOOK FOR

Your baby may make one of the motions shown here when signing
GARDEN. It may also look like she is grabbing her wrist.

Date introduced:

Date produced:

....

....

garden (version 2)

This sign may vary by region.

HANDSHAPE
O shape with dominant hand, palm up; **C** shape with other hand, palm facing you

BODY SPACE
At chest level

MOVEMENT
Move your dominant hand up through the **C** shape of the other hand, and then circle over that forearm.

MEMORY AID
This sign combines the signs for **PLANT** and **AREA**.

WHEN TO USE THE SIGN
Use this sign when going to or playing in the garden.

WHAT TO LOOK FOR
Your baby may make one of the motions shown here when signing **GARDEN**. It may also look like she is grabbing her wrist.

Date introduced:

....

Date produced:

....

Tips for signing at home

Practice signing **CRACKER**, **JUICE**, **WATER**, **CEREAL**, **PEAS**, **APPLE**, **CHEESE** and **BANANA** with your child. Teach these signs to other caregivers at home as well.

Remember, if you say any of these words, sign them! If your baby is not eating foods for the signs shown here yet, you'll still have opportunities to sign these words at the grocery store and while reading books.

Remember to sign and sing the "Baby's Eating" song when you are feeding your baby. There are at least four signs in the song and, if you feed your baby three times a day and sing the song twice each mealtime, that makes 24 times you've signed to your baby. Add four to six diaper changes with the song "Change Your Diaper" and you've reached your signing goal of at least 30 signs for the day. Anything after this is a bonus. Way to go!

Sign and sing "On Top of Spaghetti" once a day to your baby!

SIGN AND SING AT HOME

The "Baby's Eating" song is a song I made up to occupy my firstborn during mealtime. He was a very picky eater and I almost had to put on a floor show to keep him interested in eating. I originally used the words "Joshua's eating" in place of "baby's eating." Substitute your child's name for the word "baby" here as include whatever your baby is eating or drinking. Use the sign **GOOD** for the word "yum." You can find our version of this song and all the songs we share in this book on your favorite music app (search for WeeHands At Home music) .

Baby's Eating

BABY's **EAT**ing, **BABY**'s **EAT**ing

Yum, yum, yum! (**GOOD, GOOD, GOOD**)

Yum, yum, yum!

BABY's **EAT**ing **CEREAL**

BABY's **EAT**ing **CEREAL**

Yum, yum, yum!

BABY's **DRINK**ing, **BABY**'s **DRINK**ing

Yum, yum, yum!

Yum, yum, yum!

BABY's **DRINK**ing **WATER**

BABY's **DRINK**ing **WATER**

Yum, yum, yum!

Sung to the tune of "Frère Jacques"

BABY

EAT

GOOD

CEREAL

DRINK

WATER

On Top of Spaghetti

On top of **SPAGHETTI**,

All covered with **CHEESE**,

I lost my poor **MEAT**ball,

When my **DADDY** sneezed.

It rolled off the **TABLE**,

And on to the **FLOOR**,

And then my poor **MEAT**ball,

Rolled out of the **DOOR**.

It rolled in the **GARDEN**,

And under a bush,

And then my poor **MEAT**ball,

Was nothing but mush (**WET**).

SPAGHETTI   CHEESE   MEAT   TABLE

FLOOR   DOOR   GARDEN   WET

"On Top of Spaghetti" is a popular children's song that teaches functional vocabulary for some favorite foods and everyday items in your home. We've added a twist in the first verse to include a family member (see page 99 for the sign for **DADDY**, or **FATHER**). And, of course, there's that sneeze — something sure to make your baby laugh!

CHAPTER 3

Family Signs

IN THIS CHAPTER, we'll learn signs for family members, along with language strategies to help your baby learn. There is almost nothing more basic than talking about family members with babies. Who can forget that first "Mama" or "Dada"?

Keep in mind that traditionally in ASL, male signs are made on the upper half of your face, typically near your temple or forehead. Female signs are done on the lower half of your face, usually near your jawline or chin. As language becomes more inclusive you can sign **PARENT** as an alternative to **MOTHER** or **FATHER** by touching the thumb of your hand in a **5** shape to your chin and then your forehead, which combines those two signs.

Engage other family members when signing with your baby. The best way to teach your little one to sign is to have the main people in their life — grandparents, brothers and sisters — use the signs. Teaching extended family the signs for their names, for example, **GRANDMA**, may help to get those family members on board with signing with your baby. Remind them that signing with young children helps language and communication develop.

Play face to face

Encourage all family members to get down on the same level as your baby or toddler. This is the best way to see and learn more about how your baby communicates, what they are interested in and how the world looks to them. At the same time, your child will be able to watch and learn more about communicating with you. They will also love the attention when you get down and play on the floor!

Imitate

Do what your baby does! Say what your baby says! Imitate both the movements and the sounds your baby makes. Soon they will be imitating you!

Label what your baby experiences

Give your baby the names for the things that you see and do, including family members. Label those items using both signs and speech. For example, if your little one points to Grandma, say "Grandma" and sign **GRANDMOTHER**. If your baby is saying or babbling the sounds ma-ma-ma-ma, comment by saying and signing the word **MOTHER** or **MOM**.

Repeat, repeat, repeat!

Find as many different ways as possible to use the same words and signs in a day. For example, **SOCKS** on, **SOCKS** off; **HAT** on, **HAT** off; **COAT** on, **COAT** off, et cetera. The repetition will help your baby learn.

FIND THE SUPPORT

Connect with your local children's library, early years center and other community resources for new parents. Join our online community at https://weehands.community. Whether you are looking for support online or in your community, talk with other new parents who are signing with their young children when and where you can.

Most of all, make it fun for you and your child! Together you are making wonderful memories.

mother (mom)

HANDSHAPE
5 shape with dominant hand, palm facing out

BODY SPACE
At the chin

MOVEMENT
With your hand open, tap your chin twice with your thumb.

MEMORY AID
In ASL, female signs are located near the jawline. Movement at the chin indicates the female area of your face.

WHEN TO USE THE SIGN
Encourage anyone in your child's life to use the **MOTHER** sign when Mom enters the room or when saying "Mom" or "Mother" or "Mama." You'll also be able to use this sign when you come across the word "mother" in in books.

WHAT TO LOOK FOR
It may look like your baby is tapping at his chin when he makes this sign.

Date introduced:

Date produced:

....

....

father (dad)

HANDSHAPE
5 shape, dominant hand, palm facing out

BODY SPACE
Thumb touches the middle of your forehead

MOVEMENT
Hold your hand at your forehead or tap your hand twice against your forehead.

MEMORY AID
In ASL, male signs are located near the forehead. Movement at the forehead indicates the male area of your face.

WHEN TO USE THIS SIGN
Encourage anyone in your child's life to use the **FATHER** sign when Dad enters the room or when saying "Dad," "Daddy," or "Dada" or "Father." You'll also be able to show your baby this sign when you come across the word "father" in books.

WHAT TO LOOK FOR
It may look like your baby is tapping at his forehead when he makes this sign.

Date introduced:

Date produced:

....

family

HANDSHAPE
F shape with both hands, tips of thumbs touching, palms facing out

BODY SPACE
At chest level

MOVEMENT
Start with thumbs touching, then move both hands in a circle, ending with your pinky fingers touching and palms facing you.

MEMORY AID
This sign makes you think of your family circle.

WHEN TO USE THE SIGN
Sign **FAMILY** when looking at pictures of your family members as a group and when visiting them for special occasions or get-togethers.

WHAT TO LOOK FOR
Your child may initially make this sign with their pointer fingers.

Date introduced:

Date produced:

....

sister

HANDSHAPE

L shape with both hands; dominant hand facing out and other facing in

BODY SPACE

Dominant hand at the chin; other hand at chest level

MOVEMENT

Move your dominant hand from your chin to the top of your other hand.

MEMORY AID

The last movement in this sign, which starts in the female area of your face, is a modified sign for "care." A sister is typically a girl you care about.

WHEN TO USE THE SIGN

Show the sign for this word whenever you say the word "sister."

WHAT TO LOOK FOR

Your child may start this sign using only her pointer finger and moving it down.

Date introduced:

Date produced:

....

....

brother

HANDSHAPE

L shape with both hands; dominant hand facing out and other facing in

BODY SPACE

Dominant hand at the forehead; other hand at chest level

MOVEMENT

Move your dominant hand from your forehead to on top of your other hand.

MEMORY AID

The last movement in this sign, which starts in the male area of your face, is a modified sign for "care." A brother is typically a boy you care about.

WHEN TO USE THE SIGN

Show this sign whenever you say the word "brother."

WHAT TO LOOK FOR

Your child may start this sign using only his pointer finger and moving it down.

Date introduced:

Date produced:

....

grandmother (grandma)

HANDSHAPE
5 shape with dominant hand, palm facing out

BODY SPACE
Thumb touches chin

MOVEMENT
Move your hand away from your chin, making two small bounces.

MEMORY AID
The chin is the female area of the face, and the two bounces indicate another generation.

WHEN TO USE THE SIGN
Show the sign for this word whenever you say the word "Grandma," when looking at photographs of a grandmother and when she comes into the room.

WHAT TO LOOK FOR
Your baby may make this sign with more than just two bounces.

Date introduced:

Date produced:

....

....

grandfather (grandpa)

HANDSHAPE
5 shape with dominant hand, palm facing out

BODY SPACE
Thumb touches forehead

MOVEMENT
Move your hand away from your forehead, making two small bounces

MEMORY AID
The forehead is the male area of the face and the two bounces indicate another generation.

WHEN TO USE THE SIGN
Show the sign for this word whenever you say the word "Grandpa," when looking at photographs of a grandfather and when he comes into the room.

WHAT TO LOOK FOR
Your baby may make this sign with more than just two bounces.

Date introduced:

Date produced:

....

....

duck

HANDSHAPE
Bent **3** shape with dominant hand, palm facing out

BODY SPACE
At the mouth

MOVEMENT
Open and close this **3** shape (pointer, middle finger and thumb)
a few times.

MEMORY AID
This looks the bill of a duck opening and closing. Quacking
is optional but encouraged!

WHEN TO USE THE SIGN
Show this sign to your baby whenever you say the word "duck" and
whenever you see a duck, whether it's real, a toy or in a book.

WHAT TO LOOK FOR
Your child may make this sign using their whole hand.

Date introduced:

Date produced:

....

....

frog

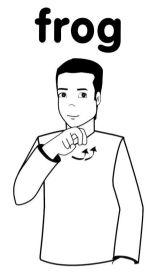

HANDSHAPE
V shape with your dominant hand, palm facing down

BODY SPACE
Under your chin

MOVEMENT
Bend and straighten your **V** fingers repeatedly.

MEMORY AID
It looks like you are imitating the throat of a bullfrog moving in and out. Sounds are optional but encouraged!

WHEN TO USE THE SIGN
Use this sign whenever you say the word "frog" and when you see a real or toy frog.

WHAT TO LOOK FOR
Your child may make an approximation of this sign by putting their hand under their chin and moving the whole hand outward.

Date introduced:

Date produced:

....

hill

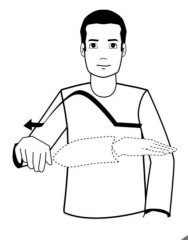

HANDSHAPE

B shape with dominant hand, palm down

BODY SPACE

At chest level

MOVEMENT

Move your dominant hand in an up and then down motion.

MEMORY AID

It looks as if you are outlining the shape of a hill.

WHEN TO USE THE SIGN

Use this sign whenever you say the word "hill" and especially when you sign and sing the "Five Little Ducks" song.

WHAT TO LOOK FOR

Your child may make this sign using a handshape that only moves up.

Date introduced:

Date produced:

....

....

day

HANDSHAPE

1 shape with dominant hand; **B** shape with other hand, palm down

BODY SPACE

Dominant hand raised, elbow on top of other hand at chest level

MOVEMENT

Move your dominant hand, pointer finger extended, down toward your other elbow.

MEMORY AID

Your dominant hand shows the sun traveling during a day and your other forearm indicates the horizon.

WHEN TO USE THE SIGN

Use this sign whenever you say the word "day" and especially when you sign and sing the "Five Little Ducks" song.

WHAT TO LOOK FOR

Your toddler may make this sign using a **B** shape with both hands.

Date introduced:

Date produced:

....

....

Tips for signing at home

Practice signing **MOMMY**, **DADDY**, **BABY**, **SISTER**, **BROTHER**, **GRANDMOTHER**, **GRANDFATHER** and **FAMILY** with your child. Remember, if you say any of these words, sign them!

Play hide and seek with baby. Have Daddy hide around the corner and say and sign "Where's **DADDY**?" Daddy can then run into the room signing and saying **DADDY** to give your child lots of hugs and kisses. Take turns doing this with different family members!

Look through photo albums with different photographs of family members. Point to the individuals in the photos, say and sign their names to baby!

SIGN AND SING AT HOME

Sign and sing the "Five Little Ducks" song with your baby or toddler a few times each day, during bath time, at mealtime and more. This is a great song to help you practice both number and family signs and teach them to your baby.

When you are signing and signing this song, sign the number of signs you are comfortable with. When you sing "quack," sign **DUCK**. Teach someone else at home the song and signs as well. You can find our version of this song and all the songs we share in this book on your favorite music app. (Search for WeeHands At Home music.)

DUCK

DAY

HILL

Five Little Ducks

FIVE little **DUCKS**

Went out one **DAY**

Over the **HILL** and far away

MOTHER DUCK said,

"Quack, quack, quack, quack." (**DUCK, DUCK, DUCK, DUCK**)

But only **FOUR** little **DUCKS** came back.

FOUR little **DUCKS**

Went out one **DAY**

Over the **HILL** and far away

FATHER DUCK said,

"Quack, quack, quack, quack."

But only **THREE** little **DUCKS** came back.

THREE little **DUCKS**

Went out one **DAY**

Over the **HILL** and far away

GRANDMA DUCK said,

"Quack, quack, quack, quack."

But only **TWO** little **DUCKS** came back.

5

4

3

continued on next page

MOTHER

FATHER

GRANDMA

TWO little **DUCKS**

Went out one **DAY**

Over the **HILL** and far away

GRANDPA DUCK said,

"Quack, quack, quack, quack."

But only **ONE** little **DUCK** came back.

ONE little **DUCK**

Went out one **DAY**

Over the **HILL** and far away

BABY DUCK said

"Quack, quack, quack, quack."

But then **NO MORE** little **DUCKS** came back.

A **DUCK FAMILY**

Went out one **DAY**

Over the **HILL** and far away

The **DUCK FAMILY** said,

"Quack, quack, quack, quack."

And all of the **FIVE** little **DUCKS** came back.

2

1

GRANDPA

BABY

FAMILY

NO

MORE

CHAPTER 4

Clothing and Routine Signs

IN THIS CHAPTER, we are going to learn ASL signs for clothing, some daily routine activities, and a new song as well as strategies that you can use at home with your child to encourage language development.

When learning a language, we are often motivated to learn the vocabulary for things that we love. As adults, we quickly learn the words for "coffee" and "wine" when visiting a country where we don't know the language. Other vocabulary and language that is important to learn are things that happen frequently in our daily routines. Some vocabulary may not be particularly motivating, but the frequency with which it is used helps us learn.

Now that you are more comfortable signing with your child with the signs and songs that have been introduced so far, you can incorporate strategies that will help with language development.

BUILDING BLOCKS OF COMMUNICATION

Three simple concepts make up what I call the building blocks of communication. They are vocabulary, turn-taking and shared attention.

Vocabulary

The activities that you have been learning and practicing so far have focused on introducing words and signs that are relevant to your baby's likes and interests. The vocabulary that you choose to use with your child should be about items or activities that are motivating as well as activities that happen frequently throughout the day.

Turn-taking

Your baby is learning that good conversations go back and forth. They are learning to take turns during interactions. Although most children are not able to share toys and take turns until the ages of three to five, children at a young age can begin to learn about turn-taking, especially in the context of a conversation. You can practice turn-taking with your little one by playing games that go back and forth, such as rolling cars or dropping blocks.

You can also practice turn-taking with your little one by imitating their sounds and movements. You may have already noticed that your baby takes turns while babbling as if she is waiting for you to make sounds back to her. Imitation games with sounds will help with speech development and imitation games with movements will help with the development of gestures and signs.

Shared attention

Another skill that children need to learn that goes hand in hand with turn-taking is shared attention. This is the ability to focus on a common activity or item with another person, for example, pointing to a picture of a fish excitedly and looking at you.

Research has shown that infants who are able to initiate more shared attention episodes score higher on language tests as preschoolers. Babies or toddlers often point to something they are interested in and make a sound that sounds like "duh." They are trying to get you to look at something they are interested in by using gesturing and vocalizing. This is communication! When you see this happen, respond appropriately. Give them the word that they don't yet know how to produce by saying and signing the word to them. By recognizing that your baby is trying to share attention with you, you can provide them with opportunities to learn.

Babies who are signed to and who can sign back have more control over the conversation and can initiate the topics they want. When a baby can get your attention by pointing to an orange and mistakenly signing "ball," that is an opportunity for you to correct her mistakes and teach her additional words. Allowing young children to play with language gives them opportunities to make mistakes. Mistakes help us learn more!

Use the clothing and routine signs shown in this chapter throughout your day with your baby. Sign and sing "Twinkle, Twinkle Little Star" at bedtime and whenever you like throughout the day.

"My baby is seven months old now. I started signing to her about two months ago and she is starting to display a few signs already!"

—SUSAN R.

shoes

HANDSHAPE
S shape with both hands palms down and held parallel to the ground

BODY SPACE
At chest level

MOVEMENT
Tap both hands together twice.

MEMORY AID
Imagine two shoes are tapping together. Think of Dorothy in *The Wizard of Oz* chanting, "There's no place like home."

WHEN TO USE THE SIGN
Show the sign for shoes whenever you say the word and when putting on your or baby's shoes.

WHAT TO LOOK FOR
Your baby may use a different hand shape when he first signs shoes. It may even look like the sign for **MORE**.

Date introduced:

....

Date produced:

....

socks

HANDSHAPE
1 shape with both hands, palms down, fingertips angled down

BODY SPACE
At chest level

MOVEMENT
With the pointer finger of both hands pointing down, brush hands against each other in an up and down motion.

MEMORY AID
Imagine two knitting needles knitting a pair of socks.

WHEN TO USE THE SIGN
Show the sign whenever you say the word and when putting on your own or your baby's socks. You will most likely have many opportunities to sign and say "**SOCKS** on"!

WHAT TO LOOK FOR
Your baby may use a different handshape when she first signs **SOCKS**. It may even look like the sign for **MORE**.

Date introduced:

Date produced:

....

coat

HANDSHAPE
A shape with both hands, hands held apart, palms facing

BODY SPACE
At chest level

MOVEMENT
Move your hands down your chest a short distance.

MEMORY AID
It looks as if you are shrugging on a coat or jacket.

WHEN TO USE THE SIGN
Say and sign **COAT** when you are putting on baby's or your coat.

WHAT TO LOOK FOR
When your baby first attempts this sign, it may look like they are signing **BATH**. Context will tell you what they mean!

Date introduced:

Date produced:

....

....

hat

HANDSHAPE
B shape with dominant hand

BODY SPACE
On top of head

MOVEMENT
Pat your head twice.

MEMORY AID
It looks as if you are showing where you place your hat.

WHEN TO USE THE SIGN
Say and sign **HAT** when you are putting on baby's or your own hat.

WHAT TO LOOK FOR
Your baby may make this sign exactly the way you do.

Date introduced:

Date produced:

....

....

sleep

HANDSHAPE
Relaxed **5** shape with dominant hand, palm toward face

BODY SPACE
At head level

MOVEMENT
Close the fingers of your dominant hand into a flat **O** shape.

MEMORY AID
The action is as if you are closing your eyes. Do this with an appropriate facial expression and close your eyes as your hand closes.

WHEN TO USE THE SIGN
Sign **SLEEP** just before nap or bedtime. Use the sign to comment when anyone is sleeping.

WHAT TO LOOK FOR
Your child may use her whole hand or only her finger moving down her face when she first makes this sign.

Date introduced: *Date produced:*

....

bath

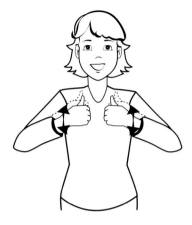

HANDSHAPE
A shape with both hands

BODY SPACE
At chest level

MOVEMENT
Move your fingers up and down at the same time.

MEMORY AID
It looks as if you are scrubbing your chest during a bath.

WHEN TO USE THE SIGN
Use the sign whenever you say the word "bath," especially before (when you are running the water) and during a bath. At the end of a bath you can sign **BATH**'s **FINISH**ed.

WHAT TO LOOK FOR
Your baby may use an open handshape at first to make this sign.

Date introduced:

....

Date produced:

....

toothbrush

HANDSHAPE

1 shape with dominant hand

BODY SPACE

At your mouth

MOVEMENT

Move your hand with pointer finger extended back and forth in a rapid motion in front of your teeth.

MEMORY AID

It looks as if you are brushing your teeth.

WHEN TO USE THE SIGN

Use this sign whenever you brush your teeth or baby's teeth. Show the sign before, during (if you can) and after the activity.

WHAT TO LOOK FOR

It may look like your baby is poking her finger in her mouth when she tries to make this sign.

A favorite rhyme I used with my children during tooth-brushing was "Up like the flowers, down like the rain. Back and forth like a choo choo train!"

Date introduced:

Date produced

....

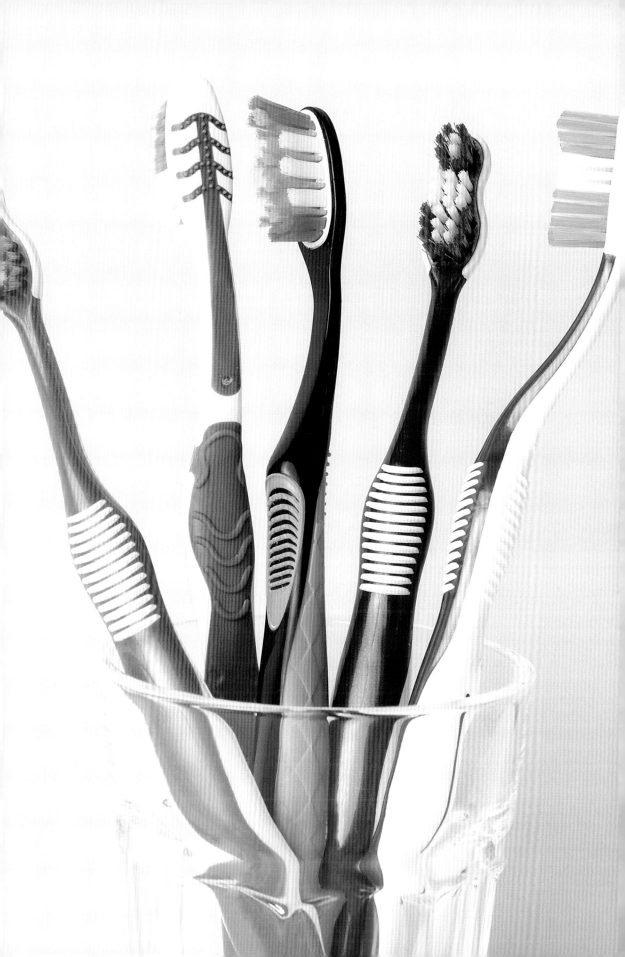

I (me)

HANDSHAPE
1 shape, with dominant hand

BODY SPACE
At chest level

MOVEMENT
Point your finger at yourself.

MEMORY AID
You are clearly pointing at yourself; also the sign for **ME**.

WHEN TO USE THE SIGN
Use this sign whenever you say or sing the words "I" or "me" to baby.

Date introduced:

....

Date produced:

....

want

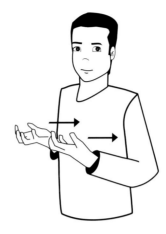

HANDSHAPE
Bent **5** shape with both hands, held apart, with palms facing up

BODY SPACE
At chest level

MOVEMENT
Pull both hands toward you at the same time, while your hand shapes change to a claw shape.

MEMORY AID
It looks as if you are bringing something that you want toward you.

WHEN TO USE THE SIGN
Show this sign to your older baby or toddler when they are signing at least one word for something they want For example, if your baby spontaneously signs **MILK**, acknowledge it. Sign **WANT MILK** and give them milk right away if you can. This way you are modeling the extra word and raising your expectations. Don't withhold something in a situation like this, though. If your baby is reaching for her milk, signs **MILK** or says "milk," they've communicated to you. Give them the item.

Date introduced:

Date produced:

....

shine

HANDSHAPE
5 shape with dominant hand, with middle finger curved forward; other hand palm down

BODY SPACE
At chest level

MOVEMENT
With the middle finger of your dominant hand, touch the ring finger of your other hand and wiggle your middle finger upward.

MEMORY AID
Imagine that rays of light are shining off the ring on your ring finger.

WHEN TO USE THE SIGN
Use this sign when you are singing "Twinkle, Twinkle, Little Star."

WHAT TO LOOK FOR
You may see your child try to make this sign by moving their hand or pointer finger upward.

Date introduced: Date produced:

....

diamond

HANDSHAPE
D shape with dominant hand; other hand palm down

BODY SPACE
At chest level

MOVEMENT
Brush the thumb and middle finger of your right hand down the base of the ring finger on the left hand twice.

MEMORY AID
You are indicating where a diamond ring would be placed on a finger.

WHEN TO USE THE SIGN
Use this sign when you are singing "Twinkle, Twinkle, Little Star."

WHAT TO LOOK FOR
Your baby may first may make this sign by pointing to their fingers or whole hand.

Date introduced:

Date produced:

....

....

star

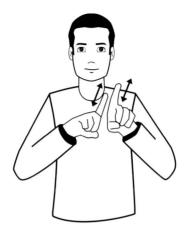

HANDSHAPE
Both hands palms forward, fingertips pointing up

BODY SPACE
At shoulder level

MOVEMENT
Brush your pointer fingers against each other in an up and down motion.

MEMORY AID
Your fingers are imitating a shooting star in the sky.

WHEN TO USE THE SIGN
Use this sign when you are singing "Twinkle, Twinkle, Little Star" and when looking at stars in books or elsewhere.

WHAT TO LOOK FOR
Babies don't always make signs correctly, just as they don't pronounce spoken words correctly. Your baby may make this sign by pointing his hands or fingers up, down or in a number of different directions.

Date introduced:

Date produced:

....

up

HANDSHAPE
1 shape with dominant hand, palm facing forward

BODY SPACE
Starts at chest level

MOVEMENT
Move your hand up once.

MEMORY AID
Your hand is moving up.

WHEN TO USE THE SIGN
Use this sign when you are singing "Twinkle, Twinkle, Little Star," when going upstairs or when a balloon floats up.

Date introduced:

....

Date produced:

....

high

HANDSHAPE
B shape with both hands, palms down.

BODY SPACE
At chest level

MOVEMENT
Raise both hands up at the same time.

MEMORY AID
It looks as if you are showing something rising or getting higher.

WHEN TO USE THE SIGN
Use this sign when you are singing "Twinkle, Twinkle, Little Star."

WHAT TO LOOK FOR
Your child may first try to make this sign by moving their hands upward. It may look like pointing up.

Date introduced:

Date produced:

....

....

world

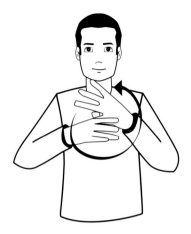

HANDSHAPE

W shapes both hands, dominant hand on top of the other

BODY SPACE

At chest level

MOVEMENT

Move hands in circular motions around each other. At first your dominant hand moves downward and your other hand moves upward.

MEMORY AID

The **W** is for world and the circular motion outlines the shape of the world.

WHEN TO USE THE SIGN

Use this sign whenever singing songs with the word "world" in them.

WHAT TO LOOK FOR

Your child may first make this sign with their whole fist instead of with a **W** handshape.

Date introduced:

Date produced:

....

wonder

HANDSHAPE
1 shape with dominant hand, palm toward face

BODY SPACE
At the side of your forehead

MOVEMENT
With your dominant hand, make small circles on that side of your forehead.

MEMORY AID
It looks as if something has come from your mind. Do this with a questioning look.

WHEN TO USE THE SIGN
Use this sign when you are singing "Twinkle, Twinkle, Little Star."

WHAT TO LOOK FOR
In place of a **1** shape, your child may use their full hand when making this sign.

Date introduced:

Date produced:

....

....

sky

HANDSHAPE
Open **B** shape with dominant hand

BODY SPACE
Starts at chest level

MOVEMENT
Sweep your dominant hand up and over your body in an arc.

MEMORY AID
You are indicating where the sky is.

WHEN TO USE THE SIGN
Use this sign when you are singing "Twinkle, Twinkle, Little Star" and when pointing to the sky.

Date introduced:

....

Date produced:

....

Tips for signing at home

Be consistent: Set a consistent example for your child. You want them to think "When Mommy and Daddy say **MORE** or **MILK**, they always sign it, so that must be how it's done." When you say a word, sign it. Babies who are signed to regularly and consistently at six to seven months of age may begin signing by their eighth or ninth month.

Repeat, repeat, repeat! Sign words for items and activities your child likes before, during and after related activities. Say and sign words for activities and items that are used frequently throughout the day as often as you can. Read books and tell stories that have repetitive language. Repetition helps the brain reinforce existing neural connections and make new ones. At the same time, repeat back sounds and movements your child makes during your playtime together.

During these activities, try to get your little one's attention and sign the words within their range of vision. Sign between your child and the object. Sign on your child; for example, tap the sign for **DADDY** on your child's forehead. Sign on objects; make the sign for **TABLE** on a table.

SIGN AND SING AT HOME

Sign and sing "Twinkle, Twinkle, Little Star" to and, eventually, with your child throughout the day and especially at nap or bedtime. You can find our version of this song and all the songs we share in this book on your favorite music app. (Search for WeeHands At Home music.)

I have a wonderful memory of my son waving his pointer fingers around and babbling during one diaper change when he was less than 10 months of age. Imagine my amazement (and how cute he was!) when I realized he was trying to sign and sing his favorite song!

Twinkle, Twinkle, Little Star

Twinkle (**SHINE**), twinkle, little **STAR**,

How **I WONDER** what you are.

UP above the **WORLD** so **HIGH**,

Like a **DIAMOND** in the **SKY**.

Twinkle, twinkle, little **STAR**,

How **I WONDER** what you are!

SHINE   STAR   I

WONDER   UP   WORLD

HIGH   DIAMOND   SKY

CHAPTER 5

More Songs to Sign and Sing

IN THE SONGS THAT FOLLOW, the key words you will sign while singing appear in all capital letters. A few new words are included in this chapter especially for these songs. You can find our version of these songs and all the songs we share in this book on your favorite music app. (Search for WeeHands At Home music.)

If you don't have a great singing voice, don't worry. If you make mistakes while signing the songs, that's all right too. Your baby or toddler will not mind. What's most important is to have fun while signing, singing and interacting with your child!

cry

HANDSHAPE
1 shape with both hands, palms facing you

BODY SPACE
Just below your eyes

MOVEMENT
Move your fingers down your face repeatedly.

MEMORY AID
It looks like tears running down your face; your facial expression matches the feeling of this sign.

WHEN TO USE THE SIGN
Use this sign whenever you say the word "cry."

WHAT TO LOOK FOR
Your baby may use their whole hand (a **5** handshape) in place of a **1** shape for this sign. That is also the sign for **SAD**. Depending on context, either sign may be correct!

Date introduced:

....

Date produced:

....

eye

HANDSHAPE
1 shape with dominant hand

BODY SPACE
Just under your eye, on your dominant side

MOVEMENT
Move the tip of your finger toward your eye.

MEMORY AID
You are gently pointing to your eye.

WHEN TO USE THE SIGN
Use this sign whenever you say or sing the word "eye."

Date introduced: *Date produced:*

....

friend

HANDSHAPE

X shape with dominant hand, palm up; **X** shape with your other hand, palm down. Pointer fingers linked

BODY SPACE

At chest level

MOVEMENT

Switch your hands so that the pointer finger that was on the bottom now is on the top.

MEMORY AID

Imagine you are showing how friends are linked together or attached to each other.

WHEN TO USE THE SIGN

Use this sign whenever you say or sing the word "friend."

WHAT TO LOOK FOR

When trying to make this sign, it may look like your child is touching their pointer fingers together instead of using **X** shapes.

Date introduced:

Date produced:

....

....

laugh

HANDSHAPE
L shapes with both hands, palms facing you

BODY SPACE
At the sides of your mouth

MOVEMENT
Move your hands up and slightly backward several times.

MEMORY AID
You are imitating the corners of your mouth moving up and down when you are laughing; use with an appropriate facial expression.

WHEN TO USE THE SIGN
Use this sign whenever you see someone laughing. Label what your baby is seeing using both speech and signs.

WHAT TO LOOK FOR
Your baby may try to make this sign at first with their whole hand, particularly when someone is laughing!

Date introduced:

Date produced:

....

....

know (knowledge)

HANDSHAPE
Bent **B** shape with dominant hand, palm facing you

BODY SPACE
At the side of your forehead

MOVEMENT
Tap your temple with the fingertips of your dominant hand.

MEMORY AID
It looks as if you are putting knowledge into your head. This is the same sign for **KNOWLEDGE**.

WHEN TO USE THE SIGN
Use this sign whenever you say or sing the word "know."

WHAT TO LOOK FOR
Your child may make this sign using a **1** shape.

Date introduced:

Date produced:

....

....

quiet

HANDSHAPE
B shape with both hands, one hand in front of the other

BODY SPACE
Starts in front of your mouth.

MOVEMENT
Move your hands down and apart.

MEMORY AID
It looks similar to the gesture for "Shhh." Use with an appropriate facial expression.

WHEN TO USE THE SIGN
Use this sign whenever you say the word "quiet."

Date introduced:

Date produced:

....

....

sign

HANDSHAPE
1 shape with both hands

BODY SPACE
At chest level

MOVEMENT
Move your hands alternately toward your body in a circular motion.

MEMORY AID
It looks as if you are sending a message with your hands. This is for the verb "sign," as in signing, not the noun, as in a traffic sign.

WHEN TO USE THE SIGN
Use this sign whenever you say or sign the word "sign."

WHAT TO LOOK FOR
Your baby's first attempts at this sign may be moving their whole hand in a circular motion, not specifically with **1** shapes.

Date introduced:

....

Date produced:

....

sing (song, music)

HANDSHAPE
Open **B** shape with dominant hand, palm down, above other forearm; other palm facing up

BODY SPACE
At chest level

MOVEMENT
Move dominant hand back and forth over other forearm.

MEMORY AID
It looks as if you are strumming some sort of instrument; also used as the sign for **SONG** or **MUSIC**.

WHEN TO USE THE SIGN
Use this sign whenever you say or sing the word "sing."

Date introduced:

Date produced:

....

....

smile

HANDSHAPE
L shape with both hands; also done with **1** shapes

BODY SPACE
At the sides of your mouth

MOVEMENT
Move both hands upward at the same time.

MEMORY AID
It looks as if you are pulling the corners of your mouth upward to smile; use with an appropriate facial expression.

WHEN TO USE THE SIGN
Use this sign whenever you say or sing the word "smile."

Date introduced:

Date produced:

....

....

then

HANDSHAPE
1 shape with dominant hand; **L** shape with other hand, palm facing dominant side of body.

BODY SPACE
At chest level

MOVEMENT
Move the pointer finger of your dominant hand from your other thumb to your other pointer finger.

MEMORY AID
This is a natural follow-up to the sign or gesture for the word "first."

WHEN TO USE THE SIGN
Use this sign whenever you say or sing the word "then."

Date introduced:

Date produced:

....

....

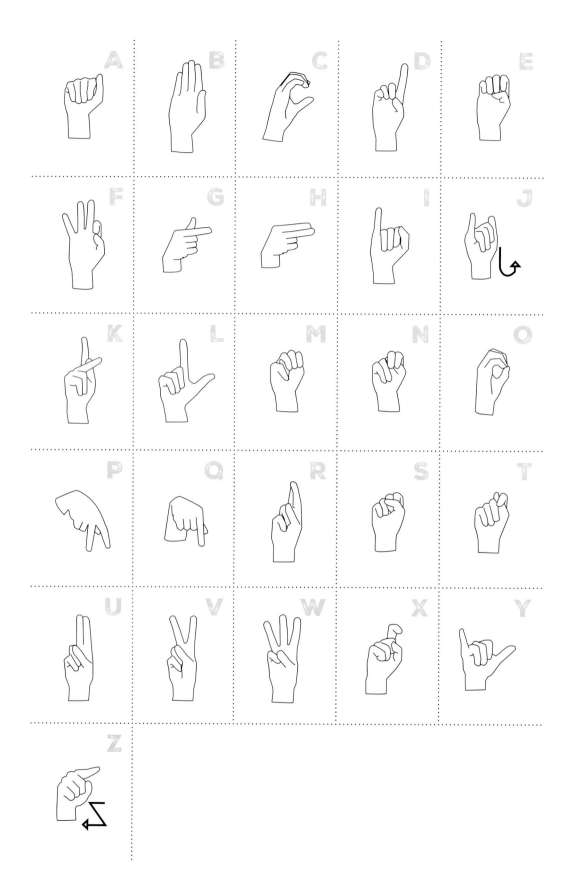

The Alphabet Song

A, B, C, D, E, F, G H, I, J, K, L, M, N, O, P

Q, R, S, T, U, V W, X, Y, Z

NOW I KNOW my ABCs.

Next TIME won't you SIGN with ME?

A, B, C, D, E, F, G H, I, J, K, L, M, N, O, P

Q, R, S, T, U, V W, X, Y, Z

NOW I KNOW my ABCs.

Next TIME won't you SING with ME?

NOW   I (ME)   KNOW

TIME   SIGN   SING

Five Laughing Babies

FIVE LAUGHing **BABIES**

Playing on the **FLOOR**,

ONE went to **SLEEP**, and

Then there were **FOUR**.

FOUR CRYing **BABIES**

Bouncing on my knee,

ONE went to **SLEEP**, and

Then there were **THREE**.

THREE HUNGRY BABIES

EATing **VEGGIE** stew,

ONE went to **SLEEP**, and

THEN there were **TWO**.

TWO happy **BABIES**

Having some fun,

ONE crawled away, and

THEN there was **ONE**.

ONE SLEEPy **BABY**,

SIGNing all done (**FINISH**),

He went to **SLEEP**,

and...ssshh! (**QUIET**) there were...none.

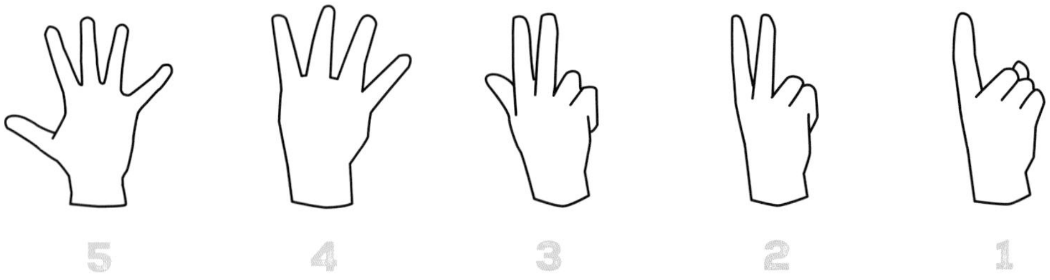

5   4   3   2   1

LAUGH

BABY

FLOOR

SLEEP

CRY

HUNGRY

EAT

VEGGIE

SIGN

FINISH

QUIET

Time to Say Goodbye

Oh it's **TIME** to **SIGN GOODBYE** to our **FRIENDS**

Oh it's **TIME** to **SIGN GOODBYE** to our **FRIENDS**

Oh it's **TIME** to **SIGN GOODBYE**

Give a **SMILE** and wink your **EYE**.

Oh it's **TIME** to **SIGN GOODBYE** to our **FRIENDS**.

TIME

SIGN

GOODBYE

FRIEND

SMILE

EYE

Sung to the tune of "She'll Be Coming Round the Mountain"

Resources

AUTHOR'S WEBSITE

Join the WeeHands online baby sign language community to connect with other parents, early childhood educators and early language development experts. We bring together parents and early development experts to learn to sign with their young children to connect with those children and reduce their frustrations so that we can have happier children and more confident parents. Visit https://weehands.community.

BOOKS ON EARLY LANGUAGE DEVELOPMENT

It Takes Two to Talk: A Practical Guide for Parents of Children with Language Delays, by Elaine Weitzman and Pat Cupples

Let's Talk, Baby, by Stephanie Ciatti

My Toddler's First Words: A Step-By-Step Guide to Jump-Start, Track, and Expand Your Toddler's Language, by Kimberly Scanlon

Talking with Your Toddler: 75 Fun Activities and Interactive Games that Teach Your Child to Talk, by Teresa Laikko and Laura Laikko

The Baby Signing Book: Includes 450 ASL Signs for Babies and Toddlers, by Sara Bingham

ONLINE SIGN LANGUAGE DICTIONARIES

ASL Signbank: aslsignbank.haskins.yale.edu

Handspeak ASL Sign Language Dictionary: handspeak.com

Lifeprint ASLU Dictionary: lifeprint.com

Signing Savvy Sign Language Dictionary: signingsavvy.com

SOCIAL MEDIA

ASL Connect: instagram.com/aslconnect

The ASL Shop: instagram.com/theaslshop

The ASL Signbank: instagram.com/aslsignbank

WeeHands: instagram.com/weehands

SPEECH AND LANGUAGE DEVELOPMENT RESOURCES

American Speech-Language-Hearing Association (ASHA): asha.org

Speech-Language & Audiology Canada: sac-oac.ca

RESOURCES FOR FAMILIES WITH CHILDREN WITH HEARING LOSS

American Society for Deaf Children: deafchildren.org

BabyHearing.org: babyhearing.org

Hands & Voices: handsandvoices.org

The National Center for Hearing Assessment and Management: infanthearing.org/index.html

BOOKS TO READ AND SIGN WITH BABY

A Potty for Me! by Karen Katz

Apples and Pumpkins, by Anne and Lizzy Rockwell

At the Beach, by Anne Rockwell

Baby Loves Spring! by Karen Katz

Big Red Barn, by Margaret Wise Brown

Brown Bear, Brown Bear, What Do You See? by Bill Martin Jr., Eric Carle

Counting Kisses: A Kiss and Read Book, by Karen Katz

Dog's Colorful Day: A Messy Story about Colors and Counting, by Emma Dodd

Good Night, Gorilla, by Peggy Rathmann

Goodnight Moon, by Margaret Wise Brown

Jamberry, by Bruce Degen

Mouse Paint, by Ellen Stoll Walsh

Oh My Oh My Oh Dinosaurs! by Sandra Boynton

One, Two, Three! by Sandra Boynton

The Animal Boogie, by Debbie Harter

The Going to Bed Book, by Sandra Boynton

The Mitten, by Jan Brett

The Snowy Day, by Ezra Jack Keats

The Very Hungry Caterpillar, by Eric Carle

Time for Bed, by Mem Fox

Where's Spot? by Eric Hill

INDEX

Note: Page numbers in **bold** type indicate the location of specific sign instructions and song lyrics.